MY DAILY PRAYER & PRAISE JOURNAL

KeyNotes

BARBOUR
PUBLISHING

ISBN 978-1-59789-831-7

Compiled by Ellen Caughey.

Published by Barbour Publishing, Inc., P.O. Box 719, Uhrichsville, Ohio 44683
www.barbourbooks.com

Our mission is to publish and distribute inspirational products offering exceptional value and biblical encouragement to the masses.

Member of the
Evangelical Christian
Publishers Association

Printed in China.

Praise be to God,

who has not rejected my prayer

or withheld his love from me!

PSALM 66:20 NIV

*Through Jesus, therefore, let us continually offer to God
a sacrifice of praise—the fruit of lips that confess his name.*

HEBREWS 13:15 NIV

New prayer requests: _____

_____

_____

_____

_____

_____

_____

_____

_____

_____

Date: _____

_____

Ongoing prayer requests: _____

_____

_____

_____

_____

_____

_____

_____

_____

_____

_____

Answers to prayer:

Praises:

And whatever you do in word or deed, do all in the name of the Lord Jesus, giving thanks to God the Father through Him.

COLOSSIANS 3:17 NKJV

New prayer requests: _____

Date: _____

Ongoing prayer requests: _____

Answers to prayer: _____

_____

_____

_____

_____

_____

_____

_____

_____

_____

_____

_____

Praises: _____

_____

_____

_____

_____

_____

_____

_____

_____

_____

_____

_____

_____

_____

Bear one another's burdens, and so fulfill the law of Christ.

GALATIANS 6:2 NKJV

New prayer requests: _____

_____
_____
_____
_____
_____
_____
_____
_____
_____
_____
_____

Date: _____

Ongoing prayer requests: _____

_____
_____
_____
_____
_____
_____
_____
_____
_____
_____
_____

Answers to prayer: _____

Praises: _____

But as for me, I trust in You, O Lord, I say, "You are my God."
My times are in Your hand.

PSALM 31:14–15 NASB

New prayer requests:

Date:

Ongoing prayer requests:

Answers to prayer: —————————————

Praises: —————————————

"He who believes in Me, as the Scripture said,
'From his innermost being shall flow rivers of living water.' "

JOHN 7:38 NASB

New prayer requests: _____

Date: _____

Ongoing prayer requests: _____

Answers to prayer:

Praises:

But He said, "The things that are impossible with people are possible with God."

LUKE 18:27 NASB

New prayer requests: _____

Date: _____

Ongoing prayer requests: _____

Answers to prayer: ⸻

⸻

⸻

⸻

⸻

⸻

⸻

⸻

⸻

⸻

⸻

⸻

⸻

⸻

Praises: ⸻

⸻

⸻

⸻

⸻

⸻

⸻

⸻

⸻

⸻

⸻

⸻

⸻

⸻

⸻

The Lord is good, a strong hold in the day of trouble;
and he knoweth them that trust in him.

NAHUM 1:7 KJV

New prayer requests: _____

Date: _____

_____
_____
_____
_____
_____
_____
_____
_____
_____
_____
_____
_____

Ongoing prayer requests: _____

_____
_____
_____
_____
_____
_____
_____
_____
_____
_____
_____
_____

Answers to prayer: ───────────────

_____
_____
_____
_____
_____
_____
_____
_____
_____
_____
_____
_____

Praises: ───────────────

_____
_____
_____
_____
_____
_____
_____
_____
_____
_____
_____
_____

Lord, thou hast been our dwelling place in all generations.

PSALM 90:1 KJV

Date:

New prayer requests: _____

_____
_____
_____
_____
_____
_____
_____
_____
_____
_____
_____

Ongoing prayer requests: _____

_____
_____
_____
_____
_____
_____
_____
_____
_____
_____
_____
_____

Answers to prayer: ────────────────────────────

_____
_____
_____
_____
_____
_____
_____
_____
_____
_____
_____
_____

Praises: ───────────────────────────────────

_____
_____
_____
_____
_____
_____
_____
_____
_____
_____
_____
_____
_____
_____
_____

Before the mountains were brought forth, or ever thou hadst formed the earth and the world, even from everlasting to everlasting, thou art God.

PSALM 90:2 KJV

New prayer requests: _____

Date: _____

Ongoing prayer requests: _____

Answers to prayer: _____

_____
_____
_____
_____
_____
_____
_____
_____
_____
_____
_____
_____

Praises: _____

_____
_____
_____
_____
_____
_____
_____
_____
_____
_____
_____
_____
_____
_____

Therefore if any man be in Christ, he is a new creature:
old things are passed away; behold, all things are become new.

2 CORINTHIANS 5:17 KJV

New prayer requests: _____

Date: _____

Ongoing prayer requests: _____

Answers to prayer: _____

_____
_____
_____
_____
_____
_____
_____
_____
_____
_____
_____
_____

Praises: _____

_____
_____
_____
_____
_____
_____
_____
_____
_____
_____
_____
_____
_____

If I take the wings of the morning. . .even there shall thy hand lead me,
and thy right hand shall hold me.

PSALM 139:9–10 KJV

New prayer requests: _____

Date: _____

Ongoing prayer requests: _____

Answers to prayer: _____

_____

_____

_____

_____

_____

_____

_____

_____

_____

_____

_____

_____

Praises: _____

_____

_____

_____

_____

_____

_____

_____

_____

_____

_____

_____

_____

_____

Seek ye the LORD while he may be found,
call ye upon him while he is near.

ISAIAH 55:6 KJV

New prayer requests: _____

Date: _____

Ongoing prayer requests: _____

Answers to prayer: _____

_____

_____

_____

_____

_____

_____

_____

_____

_____

_____

_____

_____

Praises: _____

_____

_____

_____

_____

_____

_____

_____

_____

_____

_____

_____

_____

_____

Him that cometh to me I will in no wise cast out.

JOHN 6:37 KJV

New prayer requests: _____
_____
_____
_____
_____
_____
_____
_____
_____
_____
_____
_____
_____
_____

Date: _____

Ongoing prayer requests: _____
_____
_____
_____
_____
_____
_____
_____
_____
_____
_____
_____
_____
_____
_____

Answers to prayer: _____

_____

_____

_____

_____

_____

_____

_____

_____

_____

_____

_____

_____

Praises: _____

_____

_____

_____

_____

_____

_____

_____

_____

_____

_____

_____

_____

I am the way, the truth, and the life:
no man cometh unto the Father, but by me.

JOHN 14:6 KJV

Date:

New prayer requests:

Ongoing prayer requests:

Answers to prayer: _____

_____

_____

_____

_____

_____

_____

_____

_____

_____

_____

_____

Praises: _____

_____

_____

_____

_____

_____

_____

_____

_____

_____

_____

_____

_____

What will it profit a man if he gains the whole world,
and loses his own soul?

MARK 8:36 NKJV

New prayer requests: _____

_____
_____
_____
_____
_____
_____
_____
_____
_____
_____
_____
_____

Date: _____

Ongoing prayer requests: _____

_____
_____
_____
_____
_____
_____
_____
_____
_____
_____
_____
_____
_____

Answers to prayer:

Praises:

Search me, O God, and know my heart. . .and lead me in the way everlasting.

PSALM 139:23–24 NIV

New prayer requests:

Date:

Ongoing prayer requests:

Answers to prayer: _____

_____
_____
_____
_____
_____
_____
_____
_____
_____
_____
_____
_____

Praises: _____

_____
_____
_____
_____
_____
_____
_____
_____
_____
_____
_____
_____
_____

But if any of you lacks wisdom, let him ask of God, who gives to all generously and without reproach, and it will be given to him.

JAMES 1:5 NASB

New prayer requests:

Date:

Ongoing prayer requests:

Answers to prayer: ————————————————————————

———
———
———
———
———
———
———
———
———
———
———
———

Praises: ——

———
———
———
———
———
———
———
———
———
———
———
———
———

Though I fall I will rise; though I dwell in darkness,
the LORD is a light for me.

MICAH 7:8 NASB

New prayer requests: _____

Date: _____

Ongoing prayer requests: _____

Answers to prayer: ‎

Praises: ‎

But he must ask in faith without any doubting, for the one who doubts
is like the surf of the sea, driven and tossed by the wind.

JAMES 1:6 NASB

New prayer requests: _____

Date: _____

Ongoing prayer requests: _____

Answers to prayer:

Praises:

For in the day of trouble. . .in the secret place of His tent He will hide me;
He will lift me up on a rock.

PSALM 27:5 NASB

New prayer requests: _____

_____
_____
_____
_____
_____
_____
_____
_____

Date: _____

_____
_____
_____

Ongoing prayer requests: _____

_____
_____
_____
_____
_____
_____
_____
_____
_____
_____
_____

Answers to prayer: _____

_____
_____
_____
_____
_____
_____
_____
_____
_____
_____
_____
_____
_____

Praises: _____

_____
_____
_____
_____
_____
_____
_____
_____
_____
_____
_____
_____
_____

I meditate on You in the night watches, for You have been my help.

PSALM 63:6–7 NASB

New prayer requests: _____

_____
_____
_____
_____
_____
_____
_____
_____
_____
_____
_____
_____

Date: _____

Ongoing prayer requests: _____

_____
_____
_____
_____
_____
_____
_____
_____
_____
_____
_____
_____
_____

Answers to prayer: ————————————————————

_____

_____

_____

_____

_____

_____

_____

_____

_____

_____

_____

_____

_____

_____

Praises: ——————————————————————————

_____

_____

_____

_____

_____

_____

_____

_____

_____

_____

_____

_____

But as for me, I will always have hope;
I will praise you more and more.

PSALM 71:14 NIV

New prayer requests: _____

Date: _____

Ongoing prayer requests: _____

Answers to prayer:

Praises:

Let us kneel before the LORD our Maker: for he is our God
and we are the people of his pasture, the flock under his care.

PSALM 95:6–7 NIV

New prayer requests: _____

_____

_____

_____

_____

_____

_____

_____

_____

_____

_____

_____

_____

_____

Ongoing prayer requests: _____

_____

_____

_____

_____

_____

_____

_____

_____

_____

_____

_____

_____

Date: _____

Answers to prayer: _____

_____

_____

_____

_____

_____

_____

_____

_____

_____

_____

_____

_____

Praises: _____

_____

_____

_____

_____

_____

_____

_____

_____

_____

_____

_____

_____

_____

For the mountains shall depart and the hills be removed,
but My kindness shall not depart from you.

ISAIAH 54:10 NKJV

New prayer requests: _____

Date: _____

Ongoing prayer requests: _____

Answers to prayer: ───────────────────────

──────────────────────────────────────
──────────────────────────────────────
──────────────────────────────────────
──────────────────────────────────────
──────────────────────────────────────
──────────────────────────────────────
──────────────────────────────────────
──────────────────────────────────────
──────────────────────────────────────
──────────────────────────────────────
──────────────────────────────────────

Praises: ──────────────────────────────

──────────────────────────────────────
──────────────────────────────────────
──────────────────────────────────────
──────────────────────────────────────
──────────────────────────────────────
──────────────────────────────────────
──────────────────────────────────────
──────────────────────────────────────
──────────────────────────────────────
──────────────────────────────────────
──────────────────────────────────────
──────────────────────────────────────
──────────────────────────────────────

Rejoice always, pray without ceasing, in everything give thanks;
for this is the will of God in Christ Jesus for you.

1 THESSALONIANS 5:16–18 NKJV

New prayer requests: _____

Date: _____

Ongoing prayer requests: _____

Answers to prayer: _____

_____

_____

_____

_____

_____

_____

_____

_____

_____

_____

_____

_____

Praises: _____

_____

_____

_____

_____

_____

_____

_____

_____

_____

_____

_____

_____

Sing to the Lord a new song.

ISAIAH 42:10 NKJV

New prayer requests: _____

Date: _____

Ongoing prayer requests: _____

Answers to prayer: _____

_____

_____

_____

_____

_____

_____

_____

_____

_____

_____

_____

Praises: _____

_____

_____

_____

_____

_____

_____

_____

_____

_____

_____

_____

_____

Let my prayer be set before You as incense,
the lifting up of my hands as the evening sacrifice.

PSALM 141:2 NKJV

New prayer requests: _____

Date: _____

Ongoing prayer requests: _____

Answers to prayer: _____

_____

_____

_____

_____

_____

_____

_____

_____

_____

_____

Praises: _____

_____

_____

_____

_____

_____

_____

_____

_____

_____

_____

_____

_____

_____

You shall call your walls Salvation,

and your gates Praise.

ISAIAH 60:18 NKJV

New prayer requests:

Date:

Ongoing prayer requests:

Answers to prayer: _____

_____

_____

_____

_____

_____

_____

_____

_____

_____

_____

_____

Praises: _____

_____

_____

_____

_____

_____

_____

_____

_____

_____

_____

_____

The eyes of the Lord are over the righteous,
and his ears are open unto their prayers.

1 Peter 3:12 kjv

Date:

New prayer requests:

_____

_____

_____

_____

_____

_____

_____

_____

_____

_____

_____

Ongoing prayer requests:

_____

_____

_____

_____

_____

_____

_____

_____

_____

_____

_____

_____

Answers to prayer: _____

_____

_____

_____

_____

_____

_____

_____

_____

_____

_____

_____

Praises: _____

_____

_____

_____

_____

_____

_____

_____

_____

_____

_____

_____

_____

You have cast all my sins behind Your back.

ISAIAH 38:17 NKJV

New prayer requests: _____

Date: _____

Ongoing prayer requests: _____

Answers to prayer: _____

_____

_____

_____

_____

_____

_____

_____

_____

_____

_____

Praises: _____

_____

_____

_____

_____

_____

_____

_____

_____

_____

_____

_____

_____

There is one God and one Mediator between God and men,
the Man Christ Jesus.

1 TIMOTHY 2:5 NKJV

New prayer requests: _____

Date: _____

Ongoing prayer requests: _____

Answers to prayer: _____

_____
_____
_____
_____
_____
_____
_____
_____
_____
_____
_____
_____

Praises: _____

_____
_____
_____
_____
_____
_____
_____
_____
_____
_____
_____
_____
_____

Surely the arm of the LORD is not too short to save,

nor his ear too dull to hear.

ISAIAH 59:1 NIV

New prayer requests: _____

Ongoing prayer requests: _____

Date: _____

Answers to prayer: _____

_____
_____
_____
_____
_____
_____
_____
_____
_____
_____
_____
_____
_____

Praises: _____

_____
_____
_____
_____
_____
_____
_____
_____
_____
_____
_____
_____
_____
_____

"My sheep hear My voice, and I know them, and they follow Me."

JOHN 10:27 NASB

New prayer requests: _____

Date: _____

_____
_____
_____
_____
_____
_____
_____
_____
_____
_____
_____

Ongoing prayer requests: _____

_____
_____
_____
_____
_____
_____
_____
_____
_____
_____
_____
_____

Answers to prayer:

Praises:

Lift up holy hands in prayer, without anger or disputing.

1 TIMOTHY 2:8 NIV

New prayer requests: _____

Date: _____

Ongoing prayer requests: _____

Answers to prayer: _____

_____
_____
_____
_____
_____
_____
_____
_____
_____
_____
_____

Praises: _____

_____
_____
_____
_____
_____
_____
_____
_____
_____
_____
_____
_____

Let us make a joyful noise to the rock of our salvation.

PSALM 95:1 KJV

New prayer requests: _____

_____
_____
_____
_____
_____
_____
_____
_____

Date: _____

_____
_____
_____

Ongoing prayer requests: _____

_____
_____
_____
_____
_____
_____
_____
_____
_____
_____
_____
_____
_____

Answers to prayer: ———————————————————

_____
_____
_____
_____
_____
_____
_____
_____
_____
_____
_____
_____
_____

Praises: ————————————————————————

_____
_____
_____
_____
_____
_____
_____
_____
_____
_____
_____
_____
_____
_____

Be of sound judgment and sober spirit for the purpose of prayer.

1 PETER 4:7 NASB

New prayer requests: _____

Date: _____

Ongoing prayer requests: _____

Answers to prayer: ⎯⎯⎯⎯⎯⎯⎯⎯⎯⎯⎯⎯⎯⎯

⎯⎯⎯⎯⎯⎯⎯⎯⎯⎯⎯⎯⎯⎯⎯⎯⎯⎯⎯⎯⎯⎯⎯⎯⎯⎯⎯⎯⎯

⎯⎯⎯⎯⎯⎯⎯⎯⎯⎯⎯⎯⎯⎯⎯⎯⎯⎯⎯⎯⎯⎯⎯⎯⎯⎯⎯⎯⎯

⎯⎯⎯⎯⎯⎯⎯⎯⎯⎯⎯⎯⎯⎯⎯⎯⎯⎯⎯⎯⎯⎯⎯⎯⎯⎯⎯⎯⎯

⎯⎯⎯⎯⎯⎯⎯⎯⎯⎯⎯⎯⎯⎯⎯⎯⎯⎯⎯⎯⎯⎯⎯⎯⎯⎯⎯⎯⎯

⎯⎯⎯⎯⎯⎯⎯⎯⎯⎯⎯⎯⎯⎯⎯⎯⎯⎯⎯⎯⎯⎯⎯⎯⎯⎯⎯⎯⎯

⎯⎯⎯⎯⎯⎯⎯⎯⎯⎯⎯⎯⎯⎯⎯⎯⎯⎯⎯⎯⎯⎯⎯⎯⎯⎯⎯⎯⎯

⎯⎯⎯⎯⎯⎯⎯⎯⎯⎯⎯⎯⎯⎯⎯⎯⎯⎯⎯⎯⎯⎯⎯⎯⎯⎯⎯⎯⎯

⎯⎯⎯⎯⎯⎯⎯⎯⎯⎯⎯⎯⎯⎯⎯⎯⎯⎯⎯⎯⎯⎯⎯⎯⎯⎯⎯⎯⎯

⎯⎯⎯⎯⎯⎯⎯⎯⎯⎯⎯⎯⎯⎯⎯⎯⎯⎯⎯⎯⎯⎯⎯⎯⎯⎯⎯⎯⎯

⎯⎯⎯⎯⎯⎯⎯⎯⎯⎯⎯⎯⎯⎯⎯⎯⎯⎯⎯⎯⎯⎯⎯⎯⎯⎯⎯⎯⎯

⎯⎯⎯⎯⎯⎯⎯⎯⎯⎯⎯⎯⎯⎯⎯⎯⎯⎯⎯⎯⎯⎯⎯⎯⎯⎯⎯⎯⎯

Praises: ⎯⎯⎯⎯⎯⎯⎯⎯⎯⎯⎯⎯⎯⎯⎯⎯⎯⎯⎯

⎯⎯⎯⎯⎯⎯⎯⎯⎯⎯⎯⎯⎯⎯⎯⎯⎯⎯⎯⎯⎯⎯⎯⎯⎯⎯⎯⎯⎯

⎯⎯⎯⎯⎯⎯⎯⎯⎯⎯⎯⎯⎯⎯⎯⎯⎯⎯⎯⎯⎯⎯⎯⎯⎯⎯⎯⎯⎯

⎯⎯⎯⎯⎯⎯⎯⎯⎯⎯⎯⎯⎯⎯⎯⎯⎯⎯⎯⎯⎯⎯⎯⎯⎯⎯⎯⎯⎯

⎯⎯⎯⎯⎯⎯⎯⎯⎯⎯⎯⎯⎯⎯⎯⎯⎯⎯⎯⎯⎯⎯⎯⎯⎯⎯⎯⎯⎯

⎯⎯⎯⎯⎯⎯⎯⎯⎯⎯⎯⎯⎯⎯⎯⎯⎯⎯⎯⎯⎯⎯⎯⎯⎯⎯⎯⎯⎯

⎯⎯⎯⎯⎯⎯⎯⎯⎯⎯⎯⎯⎯⎯⎯⎯⎯⎯⎯⎯⎯⎯⎯⎯⎯⎯⎯⎯⎯

⎯⎯⎯⎯⎯⎯⎯⎯⎯⎯⎯⎯⎯⎯⎯⎯⎯⎯⎯⎯⎯⎯⎯⎯⎯⎯⎯⎯⎯

⎯⎯⎯⎯⎯⎯⎯⎯⎯⎯⎯⎯⎯⎯⎯⎯⎯⎯⎯⎯⎯⎯⎯⎯⎯⎯⎯⎯⎯

⎯⎯⎯⎯⎯⎯⎯⎯⎯⎯⎯⎯⎯⎯⎯⎯⎯⎯⎯⎯⎯⎯⎯⎯⎯⎯⎯⎯⎯

⎯⎯⎯⎯⎯⎯⎯⎯⎯⎯⎯⎯⎯⎯⎯⎯⎯⎯⎯⎯⎯⎯⎯⎯⎯⎯⎯⎯⎯

⎯⎯⎯⎯⎯⎯⎯⎯⎯⎯⎯⎯⎯⎯⎯⎯⎯⎯⎯⎯⎯⎯⎯⎯⎯⎯⎯⎯⎯

But about midnight Paul and Silas were praying and singing hymns of praise to God, and the prisoners were listening.

ACTS 16:25 NASB

New prayer requests: _____

_____
_____
_____
_____
_____
_____
_____
_____
_____
_____
_____
_____
_____

Date: _____

Ongoing prayer requests: _____

_____
_____
_____
_____
_____
_____
_____
_____
_____
_____
_____
_____
_____

Answers to prayer: _____

_____

_____

_____

_____

_____

_____

_____

_____

_____

_____

_____

_____

Praises: _____

_____

_____

_____

_____

_____

_____

_____

_____

_____

_____

_____

_____

_____

Therefore I am well content with weaknesses, with insults,
with distresses, with persecutions, with difficulties, for
Christ's sake; for when I am weak, then I am strong.

2 CORINTHIANS 12:10 NASB

New prayer requests: _____

Date: _____

Ongoing prayer requests: _____

Answers to prayer: ———————————————————————

———
———
———
———
———
———
———
———
———
———
———

Praises: ——————————————————————————————————

———
———
———
———
———
———
———
———
———
———
———

Thy mercy, O Lord, is in the heavens;
and thy faithfulness reacheth unto the clouds.

PSALM 36:5 KJV

New prayer requests: _____

Date: _____

Ongoing prayer requests: _____

Answers to prayer: ─────────────────────

_____
_____
_____
_____
_____
_____
_____
_____
_____
_____
_____
_____
_____

Praises: ────────────────────────────────

_____
_____
_____
_____
_____
_____
_____
_____
_____
_____
_____
_____
_____
_____

Because thou hast been my help,
therefore in the shadow of thy wings will I rejoice.

PSALM 63:7 KJV

New prayer requests: _____

Date: _____

Ongoing prayer requests: _____

Answers to prayer:

Praises:

*But know that the LORD hath set apart him that is godly for himself:
the LORD will hear when I call unto him.*

PSALM 4:3 KJV

New prayer requests: _____

Date: _____

Ongoing prayer requests: _____

Answers to prayer: —————————————————————

_____

_____

_____

_____

_____

_____

_____

_____

_____

_____

_____

_____

Praises: ———————————————————————————————

_____

_____

_____

_____

_____

_____

_____

_____

_____

_____

_____

_____

_____

Daniel. . .continued kneeling on his knees three times a day, praying and giving thanks before his God, as he had been doing previously.

DANIEL 6:10 NASB

New prayer requests:

Date:

Ongoing prayer requests:

Answers to prayer: _____

_____
_____
_____
_____
_____
_____
_____
_____
_____
_____
_____
_____

Praises: _____

_____
_____
_____
_____
_____
_____
_____
_____
_____
_____
_____
_____
_____

Praise, O servants of the LORD, praise the name of the LORD.

PSALM 113:1 NIV

New prayer requests: _____

Date: _____

Ongoing prayer requests: _____

Answers to prayer:

Praises:

The effectual fervent prayer of a righteous man availeth much.

JAMES 5:16 KJV

New prayer requests: _____

Date: ____

Ongoing prayer requests: _____

Answers to prayer: _____

_____
_____
_____
_____
_____
_____
_____
_____
_____
_____
_____
_____

Praises: _____

_____
_____
_____
_____
_____
_____
_____
_____
_____
_____
_____
_____

For this cause I bow my knees unto the Father of our Lord Jesus Christ.

EPHESIANS 3:14 KJV

New prayer requests: _____

Date: _____

Ongoing prayer requests: _____

Answers to prayer: ⎯⎯⎯⎯⎯⎯⎯⎯⎯⎯⎯⎯⎯⎯⎯⎯⎯⎯⎯⎯

⎯⎯⎯

⎯⎯

⎯⎯

⎯⎯

⎯⎯

⎯⎯

Praises: ⎯⎯⎯⎯⎯⎯⎯⎯⎯⎯⎯⎯⎯⎯⎯⎯⎯⎯⎯⎯⎯⎯⎯⎯⎯⎯⎯⎯⎯⎯⎯⎯⎯

⎯⎯⎯

O magnify the LORD with me, and let us exalt his name together.

PSALM 34:3 KJV

New prayer requests: _____

Date: _____

Ongoing prayer requests: _____

Answers to prayer: _____

Praises: _____

He has made everything beautiful in its time.

ECCLESIASTES 3:11 NIV

New prayer requests: _____

Date: _____

Ongoing prayer requests: _____

Answers to prayer: ────────────────────

Praises: ────────────────────

Pray. . .that the message of the Lord may spread rapidly
and be honored, just as it was with you.

2 THESSALONIANS 3:1 NIV

New prayer requests:

Date:

Ongoing prayer requests:

Answers to prayer:

Praises:

God has said, "Never will I leave you; never will I forsake you."

HEBREWS 13:5 NIV

New prayer requests: _____

Date: _____

Ongoing prayer requests: _____

Answers to prayer: ───────────────

Praises: ───────────────

I will lift up my eyes to the hills—from whence comes my help?
My help comes from the LORD.

PSALM 121:1–2 NKJV

New prayer requests:

Date:

Ongoing prayer requests:

Answers to prayer:

Praises:

For you did not receive a spirit that makes you a slave again to fear,
but you received the Spirit of sonship. And by him we cry, "Abba, Father."

ROMANS 8:15 NIV

New prayer requests:

Date:

Ongoing prayer requests:

Answers to prayer:

Praises:

I will give thanks to the LORD with all my heart;
I will tell of all Your wonders.

PSALM 9:1 NASB

New prayer requests:

Date:

Ongoing prayer requests:

Answers to prayer:

Praises:

Jesus said to them, "Yes; have you never read, 'Out of the mouth of infants and nursing babies You have prepared praise for Yourself'?"

MATTHEW 21:16 NASB

New prayer requests: _____

Date: _____

Ongoing prayer requests: _____

Answers to prayer:

Praises:

I will rejoice in the LORD, I will be joyful in God my Savior.

HABAKKUK 3:18 NIV

New prayer requests: _____

Date:

Ongoing prayer requests: _____

Answers to prayer: _____

_____

_____

_____

_____

_____

_____

_____

_____

_____

_____

_____

Praises: _____

_____

_____

_____

_____

_____

_____

_____

_____

_____

_____

_____

_____